# CRIMCOMICS

## CONFLICT AND CRITICAL THEORIES

**KRISTA S. GEHRING, Ph.D.**
WRITER

**MICHAEL R. BATISTA, M.S.**
ARTIST

**CHERYL L. WALLACE**
LETTERER

OXFORD
UNIVERSITY PRESS

# DEDICATION

To Sarah Calabi,
Thank you for taking a chance on our crazy idea about criminology comic books.

To Steve Helba,
Thanks for helping steer the ship early on.

*CrimComics* couldn't have existed without either of you.

—KRISTA S. GEHRING AND MICHAEL R. BATISTA

# FOREWORD

Angela, one of the characters prominently featured in this timely comic book, makes two statements that overwhelmingly dominated sociological thinking about crime, law, and social control prior to the 1960s: (1) "[S]ociety is held together through the shared norms, values, and belief systems of people" and (2) "There is a consensus or agreement among people regarding what is right and wrong and a desire to maintain the status quo." These arguments stem from the intellectual contributions of Emile Durkheim, who is viewed by numerous sociologists as the founder of *structural functionalism*. Many sociological criminologists continue to see Durkheim as an important resource for developing their own work. In fact, regardless of how social scientists interpret his writings, Durkheim unquestionably influenced some of the most widely read and cited contemporary criminological perspectives, especially Robert K. Merton's *anomie theory*.

Today, a large and constantly growing group of criminologists pay attention to Durkheim's claims, but they respectfully reject them. These scholars, too, are resolutely sociological like Durkheim but side with Denise, another character highlighted in this comic book. As she puts it:

> I agree more with the conflict model, because I see societal beliefs as those that reflect the powerful and the dominant groups in society. There are so many different groups in society that clash with one another, and the inequities in society give rise to a variety of conflicts between groups.

It is hard to disagree with Denise when you consider recent events such as Russia's invasion of Ukraine, legislative efforts in the United States to criminalize abortion, police shootings of innocent people of color, and growing anti-immigrant sentiment spreading across many countries. Undeniably, much, if not all, of the world is experiencing urgent economic, social, and political crises, and there are signs that things will only get worse.

Though they are almost nonexistent today, some criminologists who share Denise's position are guided by *conflict theories* grounded in the work of nineteenth-century sociologist Max Weber. He was for many years considered to be one of the three or four most important classical sociological theorists. Karl Marx also belongs to this esteemed group of thinkers. While he said little about crime and law, *critical criminologists* (who also agree with Denise) drew primarily from his analyses of capitalist society from the early 1970s until the mid-1980s. Published in 1973 by Ian Taylor, Paul Walton, and Jock Young, the ground-breaking book *The New Criminology: For a Social Theory of Deviance* was especially influential in the development of *Marxist Criminology*. Most importantly, for the purpose of this book, John (another character in this issue) correctly points out that "Marx's ideas are the basis for many conflict theorists' ideas after him." Most of the conflict theorists John refers to today publicly identify as critical criminologists.

There are now at least 15 types of critical criminology, some of which are covered in this comic book, and new ones will soon appear. All critical criminologists do not think alike, follow a party line, or speak with the same voice, but as I soon point out, there are some things that bind them together. For example, while the spirit of Marx is evident in their offerings, most critical scholars today do not apply Marxist perspectives to criminological problems.

Arguably, the term *critical criminology* was coined by Taylor, Walton, and Young in their 1975 anthology *Critical Criminology*. This term has been used for nearly 50 years, but many criminologists are not exactly sure what it means. This is true not only of scholars who are not critical criminologists but also of people who are firmly embedded in the tradition. To make things more complicated, there are various definitions of critical criminology and there is no widely accepted precise formulation. If, for convenience, I was to choose a simple offering, it might be good to select this one that is very similar to the definition featured in the first edition of my book *Contemporary Critical Criminology* (published in 2011): a perspective that views the major sources of crime and social control as the unequal race/ethnic, class, and gender relations that control our society.

Many critical criminologists study the same topics as other criminologists, including interpersonal violence, criminal justice policies, drug use and distribution, and crimes of the powerful (e.g., corporate crime). Also, some critical criminologists borrow concepts from mainstream theories like *subculture* and *relative deprivation*. Still, the paramount difference between orthodox and critical criminologists is that the latter do not examine flaws in the makeup of individuals, but rather focus on the flaws in the makeup of a society that produces and sustains such people. Another key difference is that critical criminologists broaden the definition of crime to include such socially injurious behaviors as racism, poverty, sexism, imperialism, inadequate social services (such as housing, day care, education, and medical care), corporate wrongdoing, and state terrorism (e.g., torturing of inmates at the Guantanamo Bay detention camp).

Critical criminology is much more than a theoretical or political enterprise. It also involves rigorous qualitative and quantitative research on a myriad of social harms. My own empirical work involves studying various types of face-to-face and online forms of male-to-female violence using survey techniques and semi-structured interviews. Moreover, my research for the past 37 years has been, and continues to be, informed by three key strands of critical criminological ways of knowing examined in this comic book: feminism, rural criminology, and left realism. I hope you find these schools of thought as useful as I do.

I must admit that I, like all critical criminologists, do not shy away from publicly revealing my progressive politics. What is more, adhering to a long-standing critical criminological tradition, I fundamentally oppose extremely punitive societal reactions to crime like long-term incarceration and the death penalty. Instead, I, together with my radical colleagues, view major structural and cultural changes within society as essential to reducing crime and facilitating social justice. Even so, the left realist in me knows that major economic, political, and social transformations are not coming soon, especially in the United States. Thus, following in the footsteps of my mentors Jock Young and Elliott Currie (pioneers in left realism), I propose a range of short-term progressive strategies that chip away at the capitalist, racist, heteronormative, and patriarchal status quo.

In this current epoch, characterized by a rabid assault on critical thinking in and outside the academy, Krista Gehring and Michael Batista should be commended for making conflict and critical theories highly intelligible to students. Doing so with a novel comic book constitutes thinking outside the box, which is an integral part of the critical criminological agenda. Whether or not they intend to, Gehring and Batista remind us of something progressive criminologists have known for years: it is time to start thinking critically about crime. This issue of *CrimComics* is an important steppingstone toward achieving this goal.

WALTER S. DEKESEREDY
*Anna Deane Carlson Endowed Chair of Social Sciences*
*West Virginia University*

# PREFACE

I'm going to be honest—this was a difficult issue to write. The reason for this is that when I teach criminological theory, I tend to gravitate toward theories that have policy implications that can be enacted through laws and through the actions of individual actors. For example, social learning theory holds that criminal behavior is learned. This theory is the basis of effective rehabilitative programs research has shown to effect behavior change in justice-involved individuals. Social learning theory informs not only programs but also one-on-one interventions that can occur between criminal justice professionals and their clients. The theories in this issue, however, just seemed so large, so abstract, and so incredibly difficult to tackle with a program, policy, or law that I didn't know where to start or how to present the material. For example, enrolling a client in a cognitive behavioral program (based on social learning theory) is easier to do than dismantling power structures, racism, sexism, and the patriarchy. However, as Dr. Dekeseredy points out in his foreword, the theories covered in this issue are particularly salient for many individuals who are not only navigating through the criminal justice system, but who are currently living in society in general.

The inclusion of conflict criminology in this issue is to illustrate how Karl Marx's criticisms of capitalism and the conflicts inherent in that system influenced the emergence of radical criminology (later called critical criminology) in the 1970s and 1980s. There are now many types of critical criminology, and as time progresses and knowledge and experience evolve, it is likely that more will emerge. Most important, though, is that the focus of these ideas is how crime is related to inequities and power differentials found in our society. I have realized that although there may not be simple and actionable policy implications for criminal justice professionals and legislators, understanding these perspectives can help us understand the various systems justice-involved individuals occupy in our society. These perspectives can also allow us to move beyond focusing on the criminal behavior of individual actors and instead hold entities such as corporations and governments accountable for criminal acts.

There are numerous types of critical criminology, and I would urge readers to explore this criminological perspective, as they are sure to find a topic that interests them. In this issue, the types that are covered include feminist criminology, rural criminology, green criminology, left realism, conflict criminology, and peacemaking criminology. Other types of critical criminology that are not included in this issue are critical race criminology, cultural criminology, newsmaking criminology, postmodern criminology, public criminology, queer criminology, and southern criminology, to name a few.

The fact that there are so many different types of critical criminology illustrates, I hope, that it would be impossible to include all of them in this issue; however, I have included perspectives that I believe would be of interest to students and important for them to learn. This influenced how we structured this comic book; unlike in other issues of *Crim-Comics*, we did not focus on the histories of individual theorists and the development of a "family" or grouping of theories. There are, as I have noted above, far too many types in this criminological perspective to do so! Instead, readers embark on a road trip with John, Denise, Angela, and A.J., and listen as they learn about, discuss, and apply the various theories covered in this issue. It is my hope this will pique readers' interests and encourage them to explore this subject further.

As with any book project, making this issue of *CrimComics* consumed much time and effort, perhaps more so than a traditional textbook. Thinking about theory—and, in particular, trying to design a work that best conveys the theories in a visual medium—is fun. Still, with busy lives, finding the space in one's day to carefully

research, write, illustrate, ink, and letter the pages of this work was a source of some stress. We were fortunate, however, to have had an amazing amount of support during these times from family, friends, and Oxford University Press. We also want to acknowledge the talents of Cheryl Wallace, whose flair for lettering allowed us to get our ideas across to the readers.

The support of these and so many other individuals has made creating *CrimComics* possible and a rewarding experience for us. We would like to thank the following reviewers: Bill Sanders, *California State University, Los Angeles*; Elizabeth B. Perkins, *Morehead State University*; Ellen G. Cohn, *Florida International University*; Molly McDowell, *Wayne State College*; Dr. William Calathes, *New Jersey City University*. We hope that this and other issues of *CrimComics* will inspire in your students a passion to learn criminological theory.

# Conflict and Critical Theories

THIS IS IMPORTANT, A.J. VOTER SUPPRESSION SHOULD BE A CONCERN FOR EVERYONE. IT'S JUST ANOTHER WAY THE PEOPLE IN POWER USE THE LAW TO SUPPRESS, OPPRESS, AND CONTROL THOSE WHO DON'T HAVE POWER AND RESOURCES.

THAT'S WHY THIS WAS A PERFECT FINAL GROUP PROJECT FOR DR. JOHNSON'S CRIMINOLOGY CLASS.

DR. JOHNSON WANTED US TO SHOW HOW *CONFLICT THEORY* AKA *CONFLICT CRIMINOLOGY* COULD BE APPLIED TO A REAL-WORLD SITUATION-- THE RALLY IS TOTALLY PERFECT!

YEAH, WELL, I'M GLAD YOU UNDERSTAND IT BECAUSE I DIDN'T WHEN HE WAS TALKING ABOUT IT IN CLASS.

WELL, HERE'S HOW I UNDERSTAND IT: HUMAN BEHAVIOR CAN BE EXPLAINED BY EITHER THE *CONSENSUS MODEL* OR THE *CONFLICT MODEL*.

THE CONSENSUS MODEL SAYS THAT SOCIETY IS HELD TOGETHER THROUGH THE SHARED NORMS, VALUES, AND BELIEF SYSTEMS OF PEOPLE.

"THERE IS A CONSENSUS OR AGREEMENT AMONG PEOPLE REGARDING WHAT IS RIGHT AND WRONG AND A DESIRE TO MAINTAIN THE STATUS QUO."

"IF SOMEONE GOES AGAINST WHAT IS ACCEPTED OR AGREED UPON BY THE MAJORITY, THAT PERSON IS CONSIDERED DEVIANT."

I AGREE MORE WITH THE CONFLICT MODEL, BECAUSE I SEE SOCIETAL BELIEFS AS THOSE THAT REFLECT THE BELIEFS OF THE POWERFUL AND THE DOMINANT GROUPS IN SOCIETY.

THERE ARE SO MANY DIFFERENT GROUPS IN SOCIETY THAT CLASH WITH ONE ANOTHER, AND THE INEQUITIES IN SOCIETY GIVE RISE TO A VARIETY OF CONFLICTS BETWEEN GROUPS.

SO, WHAT DOES YOUR NERDY BOOK HAVE TO DO WITH THAT, JOHN?

WELL, IN THIS BOOK, MARX TALKS ABOUT THE ECONOMIC CONDITIONS THAT MANIFEST IN A *CAPITALIST* SOCIETY.

HE IDENTIFIED ECONOMIC STRUCTURES THAT CONTROL ALL HUMAN RELATIONS.

THE COMMUNIST MANIFESTO

"HE BELIEVED THAT WE COULD LEARN A LOT FROM HISTORY, AND HE OBSERVED HOW THE *INDUSTRIAL REVOLUTION* TRANSFORMED CULTURE INTO A CAPITALIST SOCIETY."

"IN THIS SOCIETY, THERE ARE THE UPPER CLASS, OR *BOURGEOISIE*, WHO OWN AND CONTROL THE MEANS OF PRODUCTION..."

"...AND THE WORKING CLASS, OR *PROLETARIAT*, WHO ARE THE WAGE-EARNERS. THEIR WORTH IS ESSENTIALLY HOW MUCH THEY PRODUCE."

"THE BOURGEOISIE DON'T PRODUCE ANYTHING, BUT THEY OWN AND PROFIT OFF WHAT THE PROLETARIAT PRODUCES."

"THE PROLETARIAT, ON THE OTHER HAND, DON'T OWN THE PRODUCTS THEY PRODUCE."

"SOCIETY IS STRUCTURED IN SUCH A WAY THAT THE BOURGEOISIE CAN BENEFIT."

"THE CAPITALIST SYSTEM'S EMPHASIS ON COMPETITION AND WEALTH PRODUCES AN ECONOMIC AND SOCIAL ENVIRONMENT IN WHICH *CLASS STRUGGLE* IS INEVITABLE."

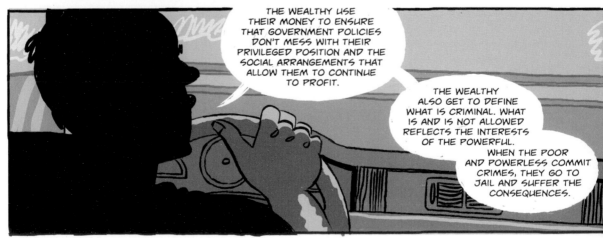

AND WHEN THE RICH AND POWERFUL COMMIT CRIMES, THEY OFTEN AREN'T PROSECUTED, OR THEY GET A SLAP ON THE WRIST.

"THE RICH GET RICHER AND THE POOR GET PRISON," RIGHT?

AH, THAT'S THE TOTAL TRUTH. RICH PEOPLE GET AWAY WITH SO MUCH-- AND IF THEY DO GET CAUGHT, THEY HAVE THE MONEY TO PAY FOR FANCY LAWYERS.

DUTCH CRIMINOLOGIST *WILLEM BONGER* WAS THE FIRST PERSON TO USE A MARXIST PERSPECTIVE TO ANALYZE CRIME.

IN HIS BOOK *CRIMINALITY AND ECONOMIC CONDITIONS* (1916), HE PROPOSED THAT CRIME WAS A FORM OF *EGOISM* THAT RESULTED FROM CAPITALISM.

"BONGER BELIEVED THAT CAPITALISM ENCOURAGES THE PURSUIT OF INDIVIDUAL SELF-INTEREST AT ANY COST. THE WEALTHY MAY USE ANY MEANS POSSIBLE-- INCLUDING ILLEGAL ACTIVITIES--TO PROTECT THEIR ECONOMIC POSITIONS."

"THEIR EXPLOITATIVE RELATIONSHIPS WITH THE PROLETARIAT DULL THE BOURGEOISIE'S ALTRUISTIC FEELINGS."

"A GOOD MODERN-DAY EXAMPLE OF THIS WOULD BE THE TRIANGLE SHIRTWAIST FACTORY FIRE IN 1911."

"BONGER SAID THE BOURGEOISIE EXPLOIT THE PROLETARIAT (WORKERS), PAYING THEM VERY LITTLE FOR THEIR LABOR AND TREATING THEM AS INSTRUMENTS TO SERVE THEIR INTERESTS."

DID YOU SEE THE NEW INSURANCE THEY CHANGED EVERYONE TO? NO DOUBT THEY DID IT BECAUSE CORPORATE THINKS IT'S CHEAPER FOR THEM.

YES, AND I CAN'T AFFORD IT. I DON'T KNOW WHAT I'M GOING TO DO--YOU KNOW MY LITTLE ONE HAS HEALTH PROBLEMS.

WHAT DO YOU EXPECT? THEY DON'T CARE ABOUT US.

"THE BOURGEOISIE CARE VERY LITTLE FOR THE NEEDS OR WELL-BEING OF THE PROLETARIAT."

"THESE LIVING CONDITIONS DEMORALIZE THE PROLETARIAT WHO CANNOT SEEM TO SUCCEED IN THIS ECONOMIC SYSTEM."

"ACCORDING TO HIM, THIS LEADS TO A LACK OF MORAL TRAINING NECESSARY FOR THE DEVELOPMENT OF *ALTRUISM* IN THE POOR."

I'M SURE A.J. CAN RELATE-- HIS EGO IS SO BIG YOU CAN SEE IT FROM SPACE!

HAHAHA HAHA HA HA HA HA

LAUGH ALL YOU WANT--THERE IS NOTHING WRONG WITH BEING CONFIDENT.

THEN OTHER SCHOLARS STARTED TO USE A MARXIST PERSPECTIVE TO HIGHLIGHT CULTURE CONFLICT AND A SOCIAL INEQUALITY PERSPECTIVE TO DISCUSS CRIME.

THIS GUY, *THORSTEN SELLIN*, DEVELOPED ONE OF THE EARLIEST CONFLICT THEORIES WITH HIS *CULTURE CONFLICT THEORY* IN 1938.

"HE SAID CRIME RESULTED FROM CONFLICTING CULTURAL NORMS."

"IN SOCIETIES WHERE THERE ARE A LOT OF DIFFERENT PEOPLE AND CULTURES, THERE ARE FEWER SHARED CONDUCT NORMS."

"WHEN THIS HAPPENS, THE LAW IS LESS LIKELY TO REPRESENT A COMMON SET OF VALUES."

SO, CRIME HAPPENS MORE IN SOCIETIES WHERE THERE ARE FEWER SHARED CONDUCT NORMS.

THAT MAKES ME THINK OF THIS CRIME THAT HAPPENED IN MY HOMETOWN. THERE WAS THIS FATHER WHO WAS FROM ANOTHER COUNTRY AND HE MURDERED HIS DAUGHTER'S HUSBAND AND HER FRIEND. THE DAUGHTER HAD CONVERTED TO A DIFFERENT RELIGION AND THE FATHER WAS VERY ANGRY ABOUT THAT.

THE FATHER VIEWED HER BEHAVIOR AS VIOLATING HIS HONOR. THE MURDERS WERE CALLED AN "HONOR KILLING."

THAT IS AWFUL, ANGELA!

I KNOW, DENISE! IT WAS REALLY SHOCKING WHEN IT HAPPENED. IN THAT CULTURE AND COUNTRY, THE KILLINGS WOULD BE VIEWED AS A WAY TO TO REGAIN THE FAMILY'S HONOR. HERE, NOT SO MUCH.

THAT'S ACTUALLY A REALLY GOOD EXAMPLE OF SELLIN'S THEORY, ANGELA.

THANKS!

CAN I BORROW YOUR PHONE?

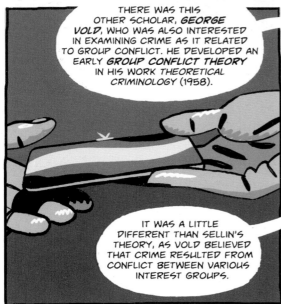

THERE WAS THIS OTHER SCHOLAR, *GEORGE VOLD*, WHO WAS ALSO INTERESTED IN EXAMINING CRIME AS IT RELATED TO GROUP CONFLICT. HE DEVELOPED AN EARLY *GROUP CONFLICT THEORY* IN HIS WORK *THEORETICAL CRIMINOLOGY* (1958).

IT WAS A LITTLE DIFFERENT THAN SELLIN'S THEORY, AS VOLD BELIEVED THAT CRIME RESULTED FROM CONFLICT BETWEEN VARIOUS INTEREST GROUPS.

HE THOUGHT THAT CRIME IS CARRIED OUT BY GROUPS FOR THE GOOD OF THE GROUP, AND THAT IT OFTEN RESULTED WHEN VARIOUS GROUPS ENGAGE IN THE STRUGGLE FOR POLITICAL POWER.

GUYS, LIVE VIDEO OF THE VOTER RIGHTS RALLY SHOWS TONS OF PEOPLE ARE THERE ALREADY.

AH I'M SO EXCITED!

SO, LIKE, LAWS ARE A PRODUCT OF THIS GROUP CONFLICT, RIGHT? LIKE, THE GROUP IN CONTROL OF THE POLITICAL POWER OF THE STATE DECIDES WHAT'S LABELED AS "CRIMINAL?"

CHECK OUT THE BIG BRAIN ON A.J.! YOU'RE GETTING IT!

"SO, THESE THEORIES DIDN'T REALLY MAKE AN IMPACT WHEN THEY WERE CREATED, BUT THERE WAS A RENEWED INTEREST IN THEM IN THE 1960s."

"THE IMPACT OF THE VIETNAM WAR ON AMERICAN SOCIETY LED MANY TO DOUBT THE CREDIBILITY AND MOTIVES OF THOSE IN POWER IN THE UNITED STATES."

"DOUBTS WERE INCREASED BY GOVERNMENTAL LIES ABOUT THE WAR. MANY MARCHED IN PROTEST OF THE WAR, AND IN MANY INSTANCES LAW ENFORCEMENT, A REPRESENTATIVE OF THE STATE POWER, REACTED VIOLENTLY AGAINST PROTESTERS."

MY GRANDMA HAS TALKED ABOUT THE COUNTER-CULTURE AND ALL THE HIPPIES DURING THAT TIME-- SHE THOUGHT IT WAS CRAZY!

"I MEAN, IT WAS A BUNCH OF WHITE, MIDDLE-CLASS KIDS DOING THINGS TO REBEL AGAINST MIDDLE-CLASS STANDARDS--LIKE, 'GETTING HIGH' AND 'FREE LOVE' WERE SOME SORT OF SYMBOLIC POLITICAL PROTESTS!"

WELL, IF YOU THINK ABOUT IT, THEY KIND OF WERE. THAT WAS ANOTHER MAJOR MOVEMENT THAT MADE CONFLICT THEORY SO APPEALING AT THAT TIME.

MY GRAND-PARENTS PARTICIPATED IN THE CIVIL RIGHTS MOVEMENT...

"...BECAUSE DURING THAT TIME, MANY WERE TIRED OF BEING DISCRIMINATED AGAINST SO THEY MARCHED TO PROTEST IT."

"POLITICAL AND PUBLIC FIGURES WERE BEING ASSASSINATED, LIKE MARTIN LUTHER KING, JR. AND PRESIDENT KENNEDY. THERE WERE RACE RIOTS IN CITIES ACROSS THE COUNTRY."

"POLICE POWER WAS USED TO SUPPRESS POLITICAL DISSENT, AND LIKE YOU SAID, THIS PROBABLY LED MORE PEOPLE TO MISTRUST THE STATE AND PEOPLE IN POWER."

YEP. AND THESE EVENTS IN THE 1960S REALLY INFLUENCED A GROUP OF CONFLICT THEORISTS TO DEVELOP AND EXPAND ON THE WORKS OF MARX, SELLIN, VOLD, AND OTHERS.

"THERE WAS LIKE A 'BIG THREE' OF CONFLICT THEORY IN THE LATE 1960S/EARLY 1970S."

THE FIRST SCHOLAR WAS **AUSTIN TURK**. HE WROTE *CRIMINALITY AND LEGAL ORDER* (1969), AND IN IT, PRESENTED A THEORY OF **CRIMINALIZATION** AND NORMATIVE LEGAL BEHAVIOR. HE PROPOSED THE IDEA THAT CRIMINALITY WAS A STATUS, NOT A BEHAVIOR. HE ALSO TALKED ABOUT CONDITIONS UNDER WHICH DIFFERENCES BETWEEN AUTHORITIES AND SUBJECTS RESULT IN CONFLICT IN CRIMINAL JUSTICE PROCESSES.

THE SECOND WAS **RICHARD QUINNEY**. A YEAR AFTER TURK, HE WROTE *THE SOCIAL REALITY OF CRIME* (1970). IN IT, HE URGED READERS TO SHIFT FROM SEARCHING FOR THE CAUSES OF CRIME TO FOCUSING ON HOW THE CRIMINAL JUSTICE SYSTEM INFLUENCES BEHAVIOR.

HE FOCUSED ON HOW THE DEFINITIONS OF CRIMINALS WERE CREATED AND APPLIED.

THE THIRD PERSON WAS **WILLIAM CHAMBLISS**. IN 1971 HE WROTE *LAW, ORDER, AND POWER* WITH **ROBERT SEIDMAN**. BUILDING ON MARXIST IDEAS, CHAMBLISS DISCUSSED HOW IN A CAPITALIST SOCIETY THE BASIC SOCIAL PROCESS IS CONFLICT BETWEEN THE SOCIAL CLASSES. THIS WAS KEY TO UNDERSTANDING HOW THE CRIMINAL JUSTICE SYSTEM WORKS.

"ACCORDING TO TURK, CRIMINALIZATION WAS THE PROCESS OF BEING LABELED A CRIMINAL. IT NOT ONLY HAPPENS WHEN SOMEONE BREAKS THE LAW, BUT IT ALSO RESULTS FROM THE INTERACTION BETWEEN AUTHORITIES (E.G., POLICE, JUDGES, LAWYERS) AND SUBJECTS. SUBJECTS ARE DISTINGUISHED FROM AUTHORITIES BY THEIR INABILITY TO MANIPULATE THE LEGAL SYSTEM. HOWEVER, NOT ALL AUTHORITIES HAVE EQUAL OPPORTUNITY TO INFLUENCE THE LAW. TURK CALLED POLICE 'FIRST-LINE ENFORCERS,' AS THEY HAD THE GREATEST IMPACT ON SUBJECT CRIMINALIZATION. CULTURAL NORMS (I.E., WRITTEN LAWS, PROCEDURES, AND WRITTEN POLICIES) AND SOCIAL NORMS (I.E., ACTUAL BEHAVIOR OR THE LAW AS IT IS ENFORCED) DETERMINE WHEN CONFLICT IS MORE OR LESS LIKELY TO OCCUR. THE ODDS OF CONFLICT ARE GREATEST WHEN THERE IS INCONSISTENCY BETWEEN CULTURAL AND SOCIAL NORMS. HE ALSO DISCUSSES **SOPHISTICATION**; THAT IS, THE ABILITY TO USE KNOWLEDGE TO MANIPULATE THE OPPOSITION. THE ODDS OF CONFLICT ARE GREATEST WHEN BOTH AUTHORITIES AND SUBJECTS ARE UNSOPHISTICATED."

"QUINNEY SAID THAT CRIME WASN'T 'REAL'--THAT IT WAS SOCIALLY CONSTRUCTED. BECAUSE OF THIS, WHAT IS DEFINED AS 'CRIME' IS DEFINED BY OFFICIAL AGENTS IN A POLITICALLY ORGANIZED SOCIETY. 'CRIME' TYPICALLY INVOLVES BEHAVIORS THAT CONFLICT WITH THE INTERESTS OF THOSE WHO HAVE THE POWER TO SHAPE PUBLIC POLICY. THIS SAME GROUP IN POWER ALSO HAS THE ABILITY TO ENFORCE WHAT THEY DEFINE AS 'CRIME,' AND THIS GROUP ALSO SPREADS THEIR DEFINITION OF 'CRIME' THROUGHOUT SOCIETY."

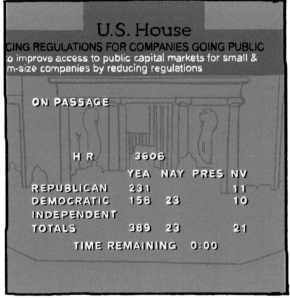

U.S. House

CING REGULATIONS FOR COMPANIES GOING PUBLIC

o improve access to public capital markets for small & m-size companies by reducing regulations

ON PASSAGE

| | | YEA | NAY | PRES | NV |
|---|---|---|---|---|---|
| H R | 3606 | | | | |
| REPUBLICAN | | 231 | | | 11 |
| DEMOCRATIC | | 158 | 23 | | 10 |
| INDEPENDENT | | | | | |
| TOTALS | | 389 | 23 | | 21 |

TIME REMAINING 0:00

"LIKE THE OTHER TWO, CHAMBLISS BUILT UPON THE MARXIST PERSPECTIVE OF LAW CREATION (I.E., LAWS REFLECT THE INTERESTS OF THOSE WHO OWN AND CONTROL THE MEANS OF PRODUCTION) BY EXPANDING IT TO THE WAYS IN WHICH THE INTERESTS OF THE RICH AND POWERFUL ARE TRANSFORMED INTO LAW AND ADMINISTRATION. IN FACT, HE PROPOSED THAT 'THE LEGAL ORDER...WAS IN FACT A SELF-SERVING SYSTEM TO MAINTAIN POWER AND PRIVILEGE.' SO, ALTHOUGH THE LAW APPEARS TO REPRESENT "PUBLIC INTEREST," IN REALITY, IT REPRESENTS THE INTERESTS OF THOSE IN POWER. FURTHERMORE, HE DISCUSSED HOW LAW ENFORCEMENT WAS A BUREAUCRATIC ORGANIZATION CONNECTED TO A POLITICAL CULTURE, AND HOW THIS CONNECTION CAN IMPACT THE USE OF DISCRETION AND RESOURCE ALLOCATION. LAW ENFORCEMENT AGENCIES ALSO PROCESS A VERY HIGH NUMBER OF INDIVIDUALS WHO ARE POLITICALLY WEAK AND POWERLESS WHILE IGNORING THE CRIMES OF THOSE IN POWER."

DUDE! YOU ARE TOTALLY WRITING OUR PROJECT SUMMARY! YOU KNOW THIS STUFF INSIDE AND OUT!

HE'S RIGHT, JOHN--YOU ARE EXPLAINING THIS WAY BETTER THAN DR. JOHNSON DID.

THIS STUFF INTERESTS ME! AND IT'S COOL BECAUSE YOU CAN SEE SITUATIONS THAT SUPPORT THESE IDEAS EVERYWHERE.

I REMEMBER DR. JOHNSON TALKING ABOUT *CRITICAL THEORY*, AKA *CRITICAL CRIMINOLOGY*, TOO...

...LIKE, IT WAS SIMILAR TO CONFLICT THEORY, BUT IT WASN'T EXACTLY.

I REMEMBER HE SAID THAT A LOT OF SCHOLARS WHO DEVELOPED CRITICAL THEORY BASED MANY OF THEIR IDEAS ON MARX, TOO. HOWEVER, CRITICAL CRIMINOLOGY WAS LIKE AN EXTENSION OF CONFLICT THEORY.

OH, YEAH! LIKE, THESE IDEAS WERE "NEW" AND "RADICAL" AND THEY CHALLENGED THE TRADITIONAL THEORIES THAT FOCUSED ON POSITIVIST EXPLANATIONS OF CRIME.

THEY WANTED TO FIND THE REAL "TRUTH" ABOUT CRIME AND THE CRIMINAL JUSTICE SYSTEM.

I REMEMBER THIS BECAUSE OF ONE OF THE SCHOLARS--HIS NAME WAS *JOCK YOUNG*.

HOW COOL OF A NAME IS THAT?

THIS IS WHAT I THINK YOU'RE TALKING ABOUT, A.J. THIS BOOK, *THE NEW CRIMINOLOGY*, WAS WRITTEN IN 1973 BY IAN TAYLOR, PAUL WALTON, AND YOUR GUY JOCK YOUNG.

WHOA--LOOK HOW MUCH THE HARDCOVER COSTS!

THE IDEAS IN THIS BOOK CAME OUT OF THE NATIONAL DEVIANCE CONFERENCE IN THE UNITED KINGDOM. IT PROPOSES THAT CONVENTIONAL CRIMINOLOGY WAS LIMITED AND A NEW FRAMEWORK SHOULD BE CREATED THAT RECOGNIZED HOW THE CAPITALIST STATE DEFINES CRIMINALITY IN WAYS THAT SERVE ITS OWN GOALS.

THAT'S COOL AND EVERYTHING, BUT IT'S ALL STARTING TO SOUND THE SAME TO ME.

CAN WE STOP SOMETIME SOON? I'M HUNGRY.

BUT CRITICAL CRIMINOLOGY IS SO COOL, ANGELA! THERE'S LIKE SO MANY DIFFERENT STRANDS AND THEY ALL CALL FOR ACTION!

OH GEEZ--IS THIS ABOUT BURNING YOUR BRA AND STUFF?

FIRST OF ALL, A.J., NO ONE EVER BURNED A BRA-- THAT'S A MYTH.

SECOND--*FEMINIST CRIMINOLOGY* IS A BRANCH OF CRITICAL CRIMINOLOGY THAT FOCUSES ON JUSTICE-INVOLVED WOMEN AND WOMEN'S EXPERIENCES WITH VICTIMIZATION. IT EXAMINES THE CAUSES, TRENDS, AND RESULTS OF FEMALE CRIMINALITY.

"THIS GREW OUT OF THE WOMEN'S RIGHTS MOVEMENT OF THE 1960S AND 70S THAT ADVOCATED FOR THE EQUALITY OF WOMEN. IT QUESTIONS THE *PATRIARCHY* AND ALL OF THE SOCIAL AND SEXUAL HIERARCHIES THAT ARE USED TO OPPRESS WOMEN."

FEMINIST CRIMINOLOGY FOCUSES ON A BROAD RANGE OF ISSUES RELATED TO WOMEN AND CRIME, INCLUDING THEORETICAL EXPLANATIONS OF CRIME, RESPONSES TO FEMALE OFFENDING, PROGRAMMING IN WOMEN'S PRISONS, WOMEN AS WORKERS IN THE FIELD OF CORRECTIONS, AND THE SPECIAL NEEDS OF WOMEN IN PRISON.

THAT'S A GROWING AREA OF STUDY, YOU KNOW-- *RURAL CRIMINOLOGY.* IT'S ANOTHER BRANCH OF CRITICAL CRIMINOLOGY.

REALLY? THAT SOUNDS INTERESTING-- ESPECIALLY SINCE TRADITIONAL CRIMINOLOGICAL THEORIES HAVE TENDED TO FOCUS ON EXPLAINING CRIME IN URBAN AREAS.

YEP. RURAL CRIMINOLOGY FOCUSES ON THE STUDY OF CRIME IN RURAL SETTINGS. THERE MAY BE DIFFERENT CRIMES THAT ARE PREVALENT OUT HERE IN THE COUNTRY, AND THE CRIMINAL JUSTICE SYSTEM MAY FUNCTION DIFFERENTLY OUT HERE TOO.

I MEAN, THINGS ARE DIFFERENT IN A SMALL TOWN. YOU TEND TO KNOW THE POLICE AND THEY KNOW YOU. SINCE EVERYONE KNOWS EVERYONE, PEOPLE OFTEN DON'T REPORT CRIMES BECAUSE NOTHING IS EVER ANONYMOUS. THERE ALSO AREN'T AS MANY RESOURCES TO HELP VICTIMS OR FUND CRIMINAL JUSTICE AGENCIES.

WHAT ARE YOU GOING TO GET?

EVERYTHING. I LOVE BARBECUE. IT REMINDS ME OF COOKOUTS WITH MY FAMILY.

I RARELY HEAR YOU TALK ABOUT YOUR FAMILY, A.J. WHAT DO YOUR PARENTS DO?

18

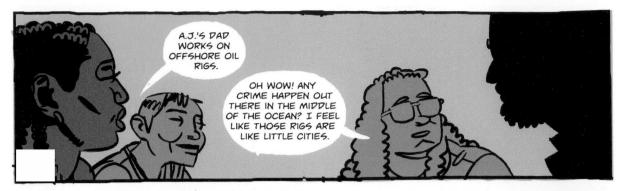

A.J.'S DAD WORKS ON OFFSHORE OIL RIGS.

OH WOW! ANY CRIME HAPPEN OUT THERE IN THE MIDDLE OF THE OCEAN? I FEEL LIKE THOSE RIGS ARE LIKE LITTLE CITIES.

I MEAN, THERE'S SOME THEFT, MAYBE ASSAULTS--BUT YOU DON'T WANT TO GET TOO CRAZY BECAUSE YOU LIVE WHERE YOU WORK, YOU KNOW?

I CAN THINK OF A CRIME THAT HAPPENED IN THE MACONDO PROSPECT-- THAT'S ONE OF THE MANY OIL AND GAS PROSPECTS IN THE GULF OF MEXICO.

REMEMBER THE DEEPWATER HORIZON DRILLING RIG THAT EXPLODED AND SANK IN 2010? THAT WAS THE LARGEST OIL SPILL IN THE HISTORY OF MARINE OIL DRILLING OPERATIONS.

THAT WAS TERRIBLE. THE SPILL WAS FOUR MILLION BARRELS OF OIL.

THAT'S SOMETHING ANOTHER STRAND OF CRITICAL CRIMINOLOGY WOULD EXAMINE--IT'S CALLED *GREEN CRIMINOLOGY.*

OH! SOUNDS RIGHT UP MY ALLEY! WHAT IS THAT?

IT'S A CRIMINOLOGICAL PERSPECTIVE THAT DEALS WITH ENVIRONMENTAL CRIMES AND HARMS.

LIKE HARM CAUSED BY GLOBAL WARMING AND CLIMATE CHANGE; HARM CAUSED BY THE HAZARDOUS TRANSPORT OF E-WASTE; ILLEGAL DISPOSAL OF TOXIC WASTE; AIR POLLUTION/ WATER POLLUTION; ANIMAL ABUSE/ RIGHTS; AND STATE-CORPORATE COLLUSION IN THE GENERATION OF ENVIRONMENTAL HARM.

I MEAN, I KNOW THAT'S ALL IMPORTANT, BUT I'M MORE INTERESTED IN COMBATING "STREET CRIME."

DENISE, DON'T BITE MY HEAD OFF

TO EACH HIS OWN. SOUNDS LIKE YOU'D LIKE *LEFT REALISM* THEN.

AH, I THINK I REMEMBER DR. JOHNSON TALKING ABOUT THAT-- WHAT WAS IT?

IT CAUGHT ON IN THE UNITED KINGDOM AND CANADA IN THE LATE 1980S AS A RESPONSE TO THE SHORTCOMINGS OF RADICAL CRIMINOLOGY (WHAT THEY CALLED CRITICAL CRIMINOLOGY BACK THEN).

THE WORK OF LEFT REALISTS TENDS TO FOCUS ON STREET CRIME, "HARD" POLICE TACTICS (LIKE STOPPING AND SEARCHING PEOPLE WHO ARE DRUNK IN PUBLIC), AND ABUSE OF WOMEN IN INTIMATE RELATIONSHIPS.

I REMEMBER DR. JOHNSON SAYING THAT THEY DID THIS BECAUSE BEFORE THE 1980S, CRITICAL CRIMINOLOGISTS WERE ONLY FOCUSING ON CORPORATE AND WHITE-COLLAR CRIME.

OH YEAH! INSTEAD, LEFT REALISTS STRESSED THE DISPROPORTIONATE VICTIMIZATION EXPERIENCED BY POOR AND MINORITY COMMUNITIES.

I THINK DR. JOHNSON ALSO SAID THAT THEY FILLED THIS GAP IN CRIMINOLOGICAL RESEARCH BY FOCUSING ON POOR AND WORKING-CLASS CRIME VICTIMS.

YEAH, APPARENTLY THAT WAS "GROUND-BREAKING" AT THE TIME.

MANY FORMERLY INCARCERATED INDIVIDUALS HAVE GONE ON TO BE PROFESSORS IN ACADEMIA. THEY'VE PUBLISHED BOOKS AND ARTICLES ABOUT THEIR PRISON EXPERIENCE. THEY HAVE "INSIDER KNOWLEDGE" IN A WAY, AND SOME WOULD CLAIM MORE CREDIBILITY WHEN IT COMES TO CRITIQUING EXISTING CRIMINAL JUSTICE POLICIES.

HUH. THAT'S INTERESTING. HERE YOU HAVE INDIVIDUALS REPRESENTING THE ACTUAL POPULATION THAT THEORIES ARE TRYING TO EXPLAIN. THEY WOULD LIKELY HAVE UNIQUE EXPERIENCES THAT TRADITIONAL CRIMINOLOGY AND RESEARCH CAN'T CAPTURE.

WELL, ALL I KNOW IS MY UNCLE CARES VERY MUCH FOR THOSE PEOPLE IN PRISON, AND HE WANTS TO DO ALL HE CAN TO REDUCE THEIR SUFFERING.

THAT SOUNDS VERY MUCH LIKE *PEACEMAKING CRIMINOLOGY.*

THAT PERSPECTIVE SUGGESTS THAT OTHER METHODS CAN BE USED TO CREATE PEACEFUL SOLUTIONS TO CRIME.

MY UNCLE SAYS THAT THE DAILY PAIN AND SUFFERING EXPERIENCED BY PEOPLE OFTEN TRANSLATES INTO ACTS OF VIOLENCE TOWARD OTHERS.

YOU KNOW, "HURT PEOPLE HURT PEOPLE."

SURE. BY SAYING THAT SUFFERING LEADS TO VIOLENT ACTS, THE PEACEMAKING APPROACH FOCUSES ON ENDING THIS SUFFERING.

THESE SCHOLARS PROPOSE YOU SHOULDN'T ANSWER VIOLENCE (CRIME) WITH VIOLENCE (PUNITIVE SANCTIONS).

GUYS! WE MADE IT! A.J., WAKE UP!

ALL THAT STUFF WE WERE TALKING ABOUT EARLIER, ABOUT CONFLICT AND CRITICAL CRIMINOLOGY, WAS ACTUALLY REALLY COOL. BUT WHAT CAN IT DO? LIKE, HOW CAN IT BE USED?

WELL, THE SIMPLE ANSWER IS IT COULD INSPIRE RADICAL SOCIAL CHANGE--LIKE, WE SHIFT FROM A PATRIARCHAL CAPITALIST SOCIETY TO ONE THAT IS BASED ON FEMINISM AND *SOCIALISM.*

WHAT'S UNIQUE ABOUT CRITICAL CRIMINOLOGISTS ARE THAT THEY ADVOCATE FOR SOME LEVEL OF DIRECT INVOLVEMENT WITH THE RANGE OF SOCIAL INJUSTICES THAT THEY EXPOSE WITH THEIR ANALYSES.

THEY WANT TO PUT THEORY INTO ACTION!

IT SEEMS AS THOUGH THAT NO MATTER WHAT STRAIN OF CRITICAL CRIMINOLOGY YOU EXAMINE, THEY ALL HIGHLIGHT THE CENTRAL ROLE OF IMBALANCES OF POWER.

I HAVE SOME IDEAS OF WHAT SOME POLICIES COULD BE! HOW ABOUT CRIMINAL JUSTICE REFORM, LIKE LEGALIZING ILLICIT DRUGS?

HOW ABOUT A HIGHER MINIMUM WAGE? OR MORE SOCIAL SERVICES AND PROGRAMS?

YEAH, A.J.! WE COULD ALSO BOYCOTT HARMFUL CORPORATIONS!

OR INVESTING IN DECENT, FULL-TIME EMPLOYMENT, INSTEAD OF SENDING JOBS OVERSEAS OR REPLACING PEOPLE WITH TECHNOLOGY?

BASICALLY, THESE THEORISTS ARE INSPIRED BY THE POSSIBILITY THAT THEY CAN EFFECT REFORMS OR TRANSFORMATIONS IN SOCIETY THAT WILL LEAD TO A MORE JUST AND HUMANE EXISTENCE FOR ALL.

LIKE US, RIGHT HERE, RIGHT NOW!

THIS ISSUE INTRODUCED THE VARIOUS PERSPECTIVES OF CONFLICT CRIMINOLOGY AND CRITICAL CRIMINOLOGY. HUMAN BEHAVIOR CAN BE EXPLAINED BY EITHER THE CONSENSUS MODEL OR THE CONFLICT MODEL. THE CONSENSUS MODEL SAYS THAT SOCIETY IS HELD TOGETHER THROUGH THE SHARED NORMS, VALUES, AND BELIEF SYSTEMS OF PEOPLE. CONVERSELY, THE CONFLICT MODEL HOLDS THAT SOCIETAL BELIEFS ARE THOSE THAT REFLECT THE POWERFUL AND THE DOMINANT GROUPS IN SOCIETY. THE CONFLICT MODEL IS THE FRAMEWORK THAT CONFLICT AND CRITICAL THEORIES ADOPT.

BOTH PERSPECTIVES RELY ON THE IDEAS KARL MARX AND FRIEDRICH ENGELS PROPOSED IN THE *COMMUNIST MANIFESTO* (1848). THEY PROPOSED THAT THERE ARE CERTAIN ECONOMIC CONDITIONS THAT MANIFEST IN A CAPITALIST SOCIETY, AND THAT THESE CONTROL HUMAN RELATIONS. THE BOURGEOISIE OWN AND CONTROL THE MEANS OF PRODUCTION, WHILE THE PROLETARIAT WORK AT PRODUCING GOODS AND SERVICES. CRIME WAS A RESULT OF UNEQUAL POWER RELATIONSHIPS AND WAS A FUNCTION OF CLASS STRUGGLE.

MANY THEORISTS EXPANDED UPON MARXIST IDEAS AND APPLIED THEM TO CRIME. WILLIAM BONGER PROPOSED THAT CRIME WAS A FORM OF EGOISM THAT RESULTED FROM CAPITALISM. THE BOURGEOISIE EXPLOIT THE PROLETARIAT AND DO NOT CARE ABOUT THEIR NEEDS OR WELL-BEING. THESE LIVING CONDITIONS ARE DEMORALIZING AND LED TO A LACK OF MORAL TRAINING NECESSARY FOR THE DEVELOPMENT OF ALTRUISM IN THE POOR.

THORSTEN SELLIN DEVELOPED CULTURE CONFLICT THEORY. HE PROPOSED THAT IN SOCIETIES THAT HAVE A LOT OF DIFFERENT INDIVIDUALS AND CULTURES, THE LAW IS NOT LIKELY TO REPRESENT A COMMON SET OF VALUES. CRIME HAPPENS IN SOCIETIES WHERE THERE ARE FEWER CONDUCT NORMS. AN EXAMPLE WOULD BE "HONOR KILLINGS" IN THE UNITED STATES.

GEORGE VOLD DEVELOPED GROUP CONFLICT THEORY. HE PROPOSED THAT CRIME RESULTED FROM CONFLICT BETWEEN VARIOUS INTEREST GROUPS.

THERE WAS A RENEWED INTEREST IN THESE THEORIES IN THE 1960S. THE VIETNAM WAR, THE COUNTERCULTURE MOVEMENT, AND THE CIVIL RIGHTS MOVEMENT WERE MAJOR EVENTS THAT CAUSED THE AMERICAN PUBLIC TO MISTRUST THE STATE AND PEOPLE IN POWER. THIS LED TO OTHER THEORISTS EXPANDING UPON EARLIER CONFLICT THEORIES. THE THREE MAJOR THEORISTS WERE AUSTIN TURK, RICHARD QUINNEY, AND WILLIAM CHAMBLISS. TURK PROPOSED THE IDEA THAT CRIMINALITY WAS A STATUS, NOT A BEHAVIOR. HE ALSO TALKED ABOUT CONDITIONS UNDER WHICH DIFFERENCES BETWEEN AUTHORITIES AND SUBJECTS RESULT IN CONFLICT IN CRIMINAL JUSTICE PROCESSES. QUINNEY SAID THAT CRIME WAS SOCIALLY CONSTRUCTED. THEREFORE, WHAT IS DEFINED AS 'CRIME' IS DEFINED BY AUTHORIZED AGENTS IN A POLITICALLY ORGANIZED SOCIETY. 'CRIME' TYPICALLY INVOLVES BEHAVIORS THAT CONFLICT WITH THE INTERESTS OF THOSE WHO HAVE THE POWER TO SHAPE PUBLIC POLICY. CHAMBLISS DISCUSSED HOW IN A CAPITALIST SOCIETY THE BASIC SOCIAL PROCESS IS CONFLICT BETWEEN THE SOCIAL CLASSES. THE LAW APPEARS TO REPRESENT "PUBLIC INTEREST," BUT IT REALLY REPRESENTS THE INTERESTS OF THOSE IN POWER.

CRITICAL THEORY, OR CRITICAL CRIMINOLOGY, IS AN EXTENSION OF CONFLICT THEORY/CRIMINOLOGY. CRITICAL CRIMINOLOGY CHALLENGES TRADITIONAL THEORIES THAT FOCUS ON POSITIVIST EXPLANATIONS OF CRIME. THERE ARE MANY DIFFERENT PERSPECTIVES IN CRITICAL CRIMINOLOGY, AND ALL OF THEM FOCUS ON AN IMBALANCE OF POWER AND CONTROL. THESE INCLUDE FEMINIST CRIMINOLOGY, RURAL CRIMINOLOGY, GREEN CRIMINOLOGY, LEFT REALISM, CONVICT CRIMINOLOGY, AND PEACEMAKING CRIMINOLOGY.

POLICY IMPLICATIONS OF THESE PERSPECTIVES CAN CALL FOR MAJOR SOCIAL CHANGES, SUCH AS REPLACING CAPITALISM AND THE PATRIARCHY WITH SOCIALISM AND FEMINISM. OTHER IMPLICATIONS INVOLVE POLICIES THAT REMOVE POWER FROM THE DOMINANT GROUPS AND EMPOWER OPPRESSED GROUPS. CONFLICT AND CRITICAL THEORISTS ARE INSPIRED BY THE POSSIBILITY THAT THEY CAN EFFECT CHANGE IN SOCIETY THAT WILL LEAD TO A MORE JUST AND HUMANE EXISTENCE FOR ALL.

## Key terms

The Communist Manifesto (1848)
Karl Marx
Friedrich Engels
Conflict Theory
Conflict Criminology
Consensus Model
Conflict Model
Capitalist
Industrial Revolution
Bourgeoisie
Proletariat
Class Struggle
Willem Bonger
Egoism
Altruism
Thorsten Sellin
Culture Conflict Theory
GeorgeVold
Group Conflict Theory
Austin Turk
Criminalization
Richard Quinney
William Chambliss
Robert Seidman
Sophistication

Critical Theory
Critical Criminology
Jock Young
Feminist Criminology
Patriarchy
Rural Criminology
Green Criminology
Left Realism
Convict Criminology
Peacemaking Criminology
Socialism

## Discussion Questions

According to Marx, capitalism is the cause of crime. If this is the case, how do you explain crime in a socialist country?

Many varieties of critical criminology have failed to offer a testable theory of crime. Given this shortcoming, can any of them be of any benefit in understanding or solving the crime problem? Explain.

What is the nature of crime in rural areas? That is, is it the same or different from crime in urban areas? Explain. How do temporal, environmental, and other contextual factors influence crime in rural areas?

Why are phenomena such as animal abuse, deforestation and wildlife poaching largely ignored by criminologists? Can such environmental crimes and harms be studied from a "traditional" criminological perspective? Explain.

## Suggested Readings

DeKeseredy, W.S. (2022). *Contemporary critical criminology*, 2nd ed. Routledge.

Lilly, J. R., Cullen, F. T., & Ball, R. (2019). *Criminological theory: Context and consequences* (7th ed.). Sage Publications.

Marx, K., & Engels, F. (2015). *The communist manifesto*. Penguin Books.

Vold, G. (1958). *Theoretical Criminology*. University of Delaware Press.